# Household Matters

## LIMITED EDITION

384 / 1000

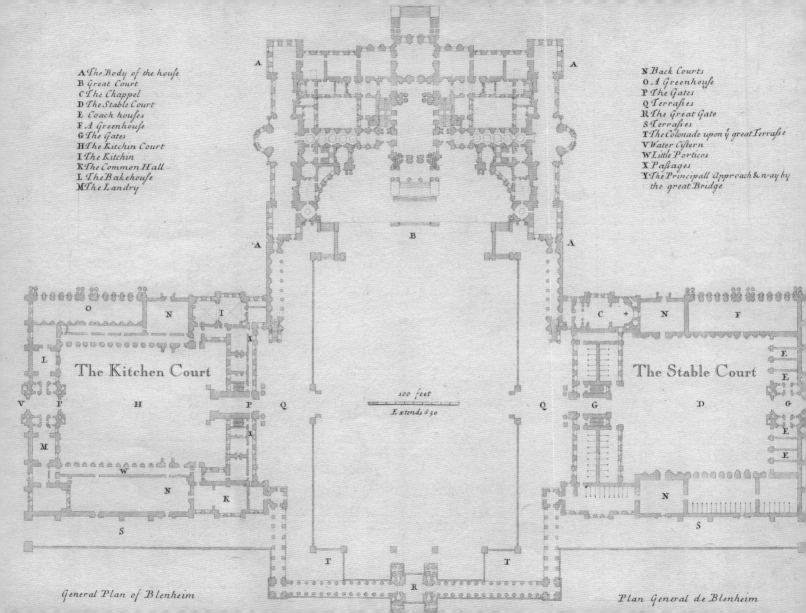

A The Body of the house
B Great Court
C The Chappel
D The Stable Court
E Coach houses
F A Greenhouse
G The Gates
H The Kitchin Court
I The Kitchin
K The Common Hall
L The Bakehouse
M The Landry

N Back Courts
O A Greenhouse
P The Gates
Q Terrasses
R The Great Gate
S Terrasses
T The Colonade upon ȳ great Terrasse
V Water Cistern
W Litle Porticos
X Passages
Y The Principall Approach & way by
 the great Bridge

The Kitchen Court

The Stable Court

100 feet

Extends 850

General Plan of Blenheim

Plan General de Blenheim

# Household Matters

## Domestic Service at Blenheim Palace

JERI BAPASOLA

# BLENHEIM PALACE

*Household Matters: Domestic Service at Blenheim Palace*

First published in the UK in 2007 by
Blenheim Palace
Woodstock, Oxfordshire
United Kingdom

The right of Jeri Bapasola to be identified as the author of this work has been asserted in accordance with the Copyright, Designs and Patents Act 1988

British Library Cataloguing-in-Publication Data
A catalogue record for this book is available from The British Library
ISBN 978-0-9502344-2-7 (hardback)
ISBN 978-0-9502344-3-4 (paperback)

Photographs are copyright of the author with the kind permission of His Grace the Duke of Marlborough, except those marked otherwise and the vintage photographs on pages 17, 44, 53, 54 and 57 which are copyright Oxfordshire County Council Photographic Archive

Cover and text design and production by
Baseline Arts Ltd · Oxford

Printed and bound in England

INSIDE COVER :
The general plan of Blenheim from *Vitruvius Britannicus*

# Contents

of the Inside Lamps

To the Chairmen for hats and Stockings ... 2 0 0

paid for sweeping all the Chimneys
being sixty six and most of them
three or four times over

A Bill to Mr. Hancock the Brazier for
Kitchin things and Laundry upon coming } 26 0 0
into the new house and several things besides

———————

102: 19: 00

**B**LENHEIM PALACE WAS BUILT in the early eighteenth century for John and Sarah Churchill, the first Duke and Duchess of Marlborough. They moved into the private apartments in the east wing in September 1719 while construction of the rest of the building was still ongoing. Blenheim was just one of several homes the Marlboroughs had at this time, the others being Holywell House in St Albans, Great Lodge in Windsor Park, and Marlborough House in London. Each house was run with the help of a few servants who were based there, along with a retinue of others who travelled from house to house, always accompanying their master or mistress.

*Marlborough House, London*

*Holywell House, St Albans*

*Great Lodge, Windsor Park*

THE 1ST DUKE ENJOYED LIVING AT BLENHEIM for just two summers before he died in 1722, and it was Sarah, the Duchess, who completed the construction and the decoration of the house even though its vast scale and cold interiors did not appeal to her. She used the house occasionally till 1735, and never returned after that, spending most of her old age at the Lodge at Windsor and Marlborough House in London, where she died in 1744.

The servants who worked for the Marlborough family in the past are by and large unidentified and forgotten individuals. However, a number of Sarah's servants are known to us through the generous bequests she made to them in her will. As Duchess of Marlborough she wielded great power at Queen Anne's court, but her outspoken and forceful personality resulted in the gradual alienation of the Queen, many of her close associates, and most of her family. On her deathbed, aged 84, Sarah was called on by just a few friends and only one of her grandsons - John Spencer of Althorp; but on the other hand, all of her most trusted servants, who had been her great consolation in old age, gathered around her.

In order to reward the most long serving and loyal of these, the Duchess left many of her servants not just well-off but wealthy. The most notable was Grace Loftus, who had entered Sarah's household in her teens as a housemaid. She remained in service for almost 40 years, during which time she married a Mr Ridley, and was widowed. At the time of Sarah's death, she was her most loyal and trusted head chambermaid.

Of all the Duchess's servants, Grace Ridley's legacy was the most generous. Her annual salary had been £10 but she was bequeathed a sum of £16,000 along with a number of more personal gifts - a striking watch, a portrait of the Duchess and a miniature

*The 1st Duchess*

*A lady's maid had a high standing in the household and the position was considered similar to a gentleman's valet.*

---

*The Duchess's hair was cut three to four times a year by a Mrs Ballion, who charged 12 – 15 shillings.*

of the Duke. A further £3,000 was given to Grace's young daughter Anne, who lived with her, to be paid to her on marriage. As was the custom at the time, Mrs Ridley received half of Sarah's clothes; with quarter shares given to each of her other two maids, Anne Patten and Olive Loft. They also received annual cash payments of £130 and £40 respectively.

James Stephens, the Duchess's secretary, was liberally gifted a substantial cash sum of £13,000, an annuity of £300 and was permitted to remain in the apartment he occupied at Marlborough House in London.

Other loyal servants were also left substantial bequests:

| Name | Position | Annual salary | Annual bequest |
| --- | --- | --- | --- |
| **John Griffiths** | *Butler* | £15 | £200 |
| **Elizabeth Arbour** | *Housekeeper* | £10 | £200 |
| **Jeremiah Lewis** | *Groom of the Chambers* | £15 | £50 |
| **John Dorset** | *Coachman* | £8 | £50 |
| **Walter Jones** | *Porter* | £8 | £30 |
| **George Humphries** | *Chairman* | – | £20 |
| **John Robins** | *Chairman* | – | £20 |

This was generosity on a scale never to be witnessed again in the family's history. When Susan, wife of the 5th Duke, died a century later in 1841, she left Mrs Haven and Mrs Rumbold, members of her personal staff, 10 guineas each.

A

# TRUE COPY

OF THE

## Last Will and Testament

OF HER GRACE

SARAH, late Dutchess Dowager of MARLBOROUGH.

THIS is the last Will and Testament of me, Sarah, Dutchess Dowager of Marlborough, made this 11th Day of August, in the Year of our Lord 1744. First, My Will and Desire is, that I may be buried at Blenheim, near the Body of my dear Husband John, late Duke of Marlborough; and if I die before his Body is removed thither, I desire Francis, Earl Godolphin, to direct the same to be removed to Blenheim aforesaid, as was always intended.

A 3                    And.

© Private Collection

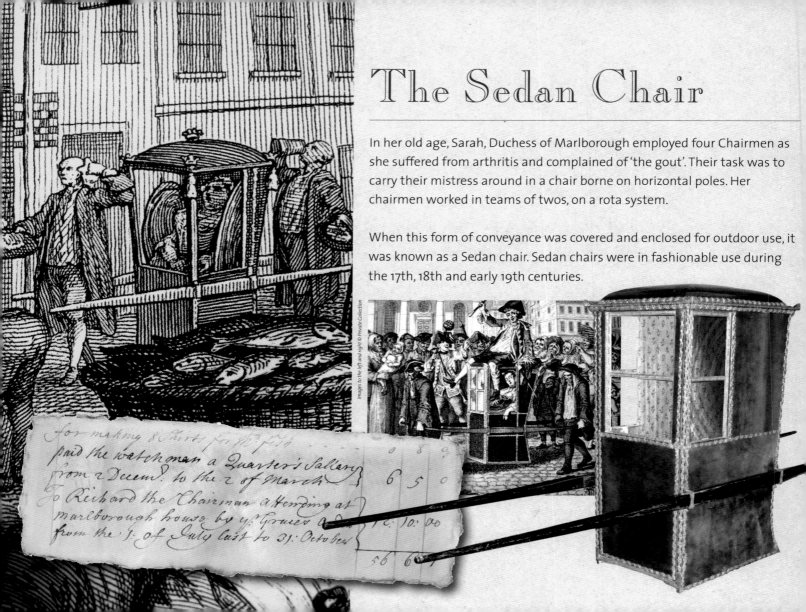

# The Sedan Chair

In her old age, Sarah, Duchess of Marlborough employed four Chairmen as she suffered from arthritis and complained of 'the gout'. Their task was to carry their mistress around in a chair borne on horizontal poles. Her chairmen worked in teams of twos, on a rota system.

When this form of conveyance was covered and enclosed for outdoor use, it was known as a Sedan chair. Sedan chairs were in fashionable use during the 17th, 18th and early 19th centuries.

*This is the most important portrait in the Blenheim collection in which a servant is included.*
*John Churchill, 1st Duke of Marlborough was a great military leader who commanded the English and allied forces in the War of the Spanish Succession (1702–13).*
*His black page, pictured here, is known to have accompanied the Duke on the battlefield in both 1704 and 1706, when the great victories at Blenheim and Ramillies were achieved. In this portrait, the Duke's page is shown wearing a red coat, similar in colour to the English army uniform. The silver collar round his neck was a sign of ownership. At this time it was still fashionable for wealthy and important families to have black servants, and their inclusion in family portraits was a symbol of affluence, luxury, and power.*

More recently in 1964, when the American heiress, Consuelo Vanderbilt, first wife of the 9th Duke of Marlborough died, she left her butler Louis Hoffmann £14,200, while his wife, Lucienne, who was also in Consuelo's service, received £5,350.

Apart from her extraordinary generosity, the 1st Duchess's will reveals the wide gap that existed between upper and lower servants. Upper servants like James Stephens (her secretary) and Walter Jones (her porter) were educated and held in great trust and regard. Stephens was a D.Med from Oxford and was privy to the Duchess's financial and legal business for over thirty years, while Jones *"has had so good an education that I employ him to coppie many papers, which is of great use, for he writes a very good hand and very good English..."*

Equally trusted, Grace Ridley looked after all her mistress's personal requirements and was provided with her own rooms in each of the family's houses. At Blenheim, her room was on a mezzanine floor above the Duchess's bedchamber. It was furnished with a blue curtained bedstead, a mattress, bolster, featherbed, three blankets, a pillow, and a white tufted counterpane. There was also a wooden table, a mirror and three chairs. The room had a fireplace. This manner of furnishing was typical of all the upper servants' rooms.

The male servants of the bedchamber, who waited on the 1st Duke during the short periods he spent at Blenheim, were accommodated in small rooms in a separate mezzanine above the principal floor.

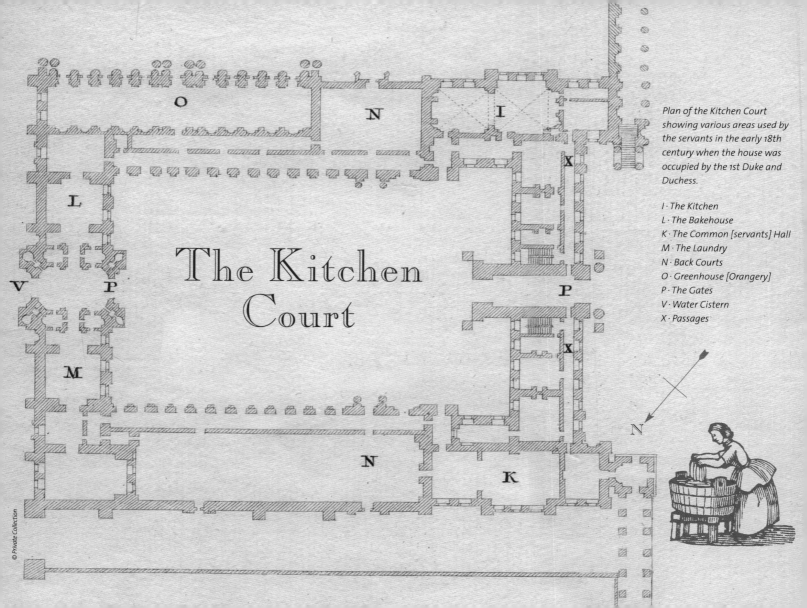

# The Kitchen Court

O

N

I

L

X

V

P

P

X

M

N

K

N

Plan of the Kitchen Court showing various areas used by the servants in the early 18th century when the house was occupied by the 1st Duke and Duchess.

I · The Kitchen
L · The Bakehouse
K · The Common [servants] Hall
M · The Laundry
N · Back Courts
O · Greenhouse [Orangery]
P · The Gates
V · Water Cistern
X · Passages

The laundry, the drying yard and ironing rooms occupied a large section of the north east corner of the Kitchen Court. In the yard there were 27 posts strung up with wire lines, whilst four clothes horses, six double horses, 24 flat irons, two box irons, two hanging irons and five ironing tables were used in the laundry and adjacent ironing rooms.

Diagonally opposite the laundry was the large kitchen which was also well equipped. The inventory included 16 saucepans, two fish kettles, two porridge pots, brass spoons, skimmers and slices, 20 pewter dishes, 11 pewter plates, four iron dripping pans, four frying pans and a variety of knives, cleavers, forks, ladles, tongs and spits. The food was cooked on two large ranges with iron backs which had hooks and fitted racks. There were fenders, pokers and shovels to hand. Four elm dressers were placed around the kitchen walls and there was also an ash dresser with shelves and three chairs for the servants. The cook was supplied with an hour glass, a salt box and a mortar and pestle. The kitchen windows were dressed with coarse linen curtains. In the corridor outside the kitchen was a large pair of iron-beamed scales with weights.

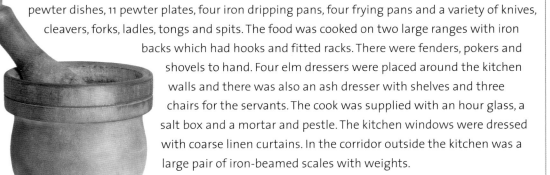

# Livery

**Livery stands for the clothes of a manservant delivered to him by his master. This is distinctive clothing worn by the servants of a person of rank and standing.**

The following extract is taken from Sarah, Duchess of Marlborough's account of her servants in the early 18th century:

"*Grooms and country porters and men that clean the courts and light the lamps have only plain liveries: and the footmen have likewise plain liveries for summer and frocks to use in the morning when they do business. Once a year or whenever they have liveries made, they have 20 shillings a piece to buy them hats, shoes and stockings... If you make laced liveries or anything for the town, they are laid by when you go into the country and consequently last very well two winters... Laced liveries should be no more than coach men, postilion, porter and footmen which may be seven or eight, and that number will require laced liveries once in two years and great coats and plain liveries every year.*

*The cloth for these liveries is four yards each. Mr Nash furnishes me with that for eight shillings a yard, better cloth than I have ever had of the drapers for ten. ... Tailor's bill for making a plain livery for a footman is £1:18:0, for a stableman £1:8:0. Lining is 7½ yards of shalloon for each at 1s:6d a yard. Plush breeches take up 2½ yards each at 5s:3d a yard. Leather breeches cost a guinea a pair. ... Making a chairman's livery is £1:12:0. ... Laced liveries come to about £4 more than plain ones.*"

© Blenheim Palace to left and right

*The East Tower, now the main visitor entrance to Blenheim. In the early 18th century, the top of this tower contained a huge lead cistern which supplied water to the east wing of the house.* ◄

*Old lead drainage pipes decorated with the cipher of the Duke of Marlborough* ◄◄

The kitchen was sited well away from the main house as owners of country houses were always conscious of the risk of fire. In the early 18th century, fires had to be put out by the servants who worked there. Water from the river Glyme in the valley below was pumped up to a huge cistern installed in the east tower of the Kitchen Court from where the east wing of the house was supplied through lead pipes. A hand pump called the "fire engine", 98 leather buckets, and leather pipes were stored in the passages around the kitchen and the bakehouse.

The servant's hall was furnished with five benches placed around two large tables. A salt box and a towel roll were also provided. The butler had two fully furnished rooms. He was also in charge of the wine cellars where there were 43 hogsheads, 57 pips, and 20 barrels in store.

House design had changed by the late Stuart period, when Blenheim was being built. The corridor was then a new invention which allowed servants to move around without being seen. The gap between master and servant was steadily widening in every sense and would eventually become an unbridgeable gulf.

The cook, the butler and the housekeeper, who formed part of the upper household, had their rooms in the Kitchen Court. Initially, the cook at Blenheim was a Mrs Foulkes, who was assisted by a single kitchen maid. Subsequently, from the mid- 18th century, the head cook was always a man.

*Servants' staircases within the house and in the service courts* ◄ ▲

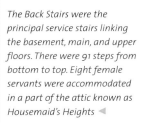

*The Back Stairs were the principal service stairs linking the basement, main, and upper floors. There were 91 steps from bottom to top. Eight female servants were accommodated in a part of the attic known as Housemaid's Heights* ◀

*Servants' rooms in the attics, now long unoccupied* ◀ ◀ ▶

Lower servants, such as maids and footmen, slept in garret rooms at the very top of the main body of the house. Four men slept in the Footmen's Tower [Postilion Heights] while eight women were housed in the Maid's Tower [Housemaid's Heights], with provision for four more maids in another part of the attic storey. Small, precisely formed service staircases, made from either stone or wood, led to convenient points on different floors or sometimes between storeys from which servants could enter and exit without being seen.

## Well looked after

*Sarah, the 1st Duchess, was a caring employer – all her servants were provided with featherbeds and linen towels. If they fell ill, they were nursed back to health and given free medicines. If they died in service, the funeral was paid for and their wage, often with a generous extra amount added, was given to their next of kin.*

The laundry maids, baker and gate keeper were lodged in the Kitchen Court, above their places of work. Day workers were also hired when members of staff fell ill or when extra hands were needed. Coachmen, grooms and stable boys had their rooms in the Stable Court. This part of the building was, unfortunately, never entirely completed.

The service wings, designed on a monumental scale by John Vanbrugh, Blenheim's architect, were intended to enhance the magnitude and prestige of the house, and thereby of its owners. The design of the service courts specifically kept staff out of sight from the main house. The outer windows at ground level were placed so high that servants would not be able to look out of them, ensuring that their masters would never catch sight of them as they went about their routines.

*The windows of the Kitchen Court which overlooked the Great Court in front of the house were placed so high that servants would not be seen going about their routines nor would they be able to look out of them* ▲ ▶

# Coachmen at Blenheim Palace

A Blenheim Palace coachman c. 1900, in full livery with his whip. ▶

Similar livery is on display in the Palace today ▶▶▼

© Private Collection

Painting of a Bay Hunter held by a Groom, attributed to John Barwick. This is the only picture of a groom in the Blenheim collection, though his face is hidden. ▶

1758-1817
A peak in activity

*I*N THE SECOND HALF of the eighteenth century, when George Spencer inherited the title as the 4th Duke of Marlborough, he decided to make Blenheim his principal home. This decision revitalized the house, and for the first time in its history it was occupied by a young and expanding family. Rooms above the Kitchen Court and in the attics were fully occupied as the numbers of servants increased steadily through these years.

*The 4th Duke*

THE 4TH DUKE EMPLOYED SERVANTS not only at Blenheim but also at his numerous other houses. These included Marlborough House in London, Blandford Lodge, Sion Hill House in Ealing, Langley near Slough, another Marlborough House in Brighton, Parkbury Lodge at St. Albans, and a town house in Oxford, all of which were owned and occupied at various times through his tenure, which lasted almost 60 years.

With a growing family of young children to be accommodated, educated, fed and generally looked after the number of staff multiplied accordingly. Servants always greatly outnumbered the family.

When in 1764, the household consisted of just two children, staff numbers stood at 91, of which 72 were employed at Blenheim, and 39 of these worked indoors.

*The 4th Duke's children in 1777*

*Marlborough House, Brighton*

*Langley, near Slough*

By 1775, when six of the Duke's children had been born, the total number of staff had risen to 102, of which 90 were at Blenheim, 54 of these working indoors.

By 1785 all eight children had been born, but the records for 1789 and 1795 show that staff numbers remained almost level, at 52 and 48 indoor servants respectively.

## By 1775 the total number of staff employed had risen to 102

The steward's account for 1775 reveals interesting information regarding the organization and running of the household at Blenheim. Lord Blandford, the Duke's eldest son and heir to the title, already had his own footman and his own cook at the age of just nine; while his younger brother, Lord Henry, aged five, had his own chambermaid. In the nursery, there were two nurses and a nursery maid. A French governess was employed by the Duke to educate his children, while for his wife Caroline, Duchess of Marlborough, a French hairdresser was engaged to create the highly fantastical hairstyles then in fashion.

# Personal servants

*In 1772, the 4th Duke had a valet and two designated footmen but the Duchess (left) had a larger number of personal staff – a lady's maid, two housemaids and three footmen. In addition, a Frenchman called Rodet was employed as her personal hairdresser from the 27th of February 1772. By 1775 he had been replaced by a Monsieur Messureur. Both these French hairdressers earned £42 annually and ranked amongst the higher paid staff in the household.*

*An 18th-century engraving of a hairdresser creating a fashionable hairstyle*

© Private Collection

With such large numbers involved, feeding the family as well as all the servants was a major operation. The records for 1775 also reveal the organisation and hierarchy of the kitchen staff:

| Servant's name | Position | Annual wage £:s |
|---|---|---|
| John Read | Clerk of the Kitchen & Confectioner | 80:00 |
| Thomas Mileham | Cook | 73:10 |
| James Beckley | Second Cook | 31:10 |
| Elizabeth Thomas | Lord Blandford's Cook | 12:00 |
| William Gale | Baker | 25:00 |
| Jane Gray | Kitchen maid | 8:00 |
| Diana Cooper | Still room maid | 6:00 |
| Mary Meredith | Confectionery Maid | 9:03 |
| Thomas Pearce | Kitchen Man | 8:00 |

The lower servants were responsible for preparing ingredients for the cook as well as the servants' meals.

*In large country houses there was a clear hierarchy of servants where everybody 'knew their place'. The lower servants performed the bulk of the hard physical labour while the upper servants had more of a supervisory role ▶*

*Details of the engraving ('M' for Marlborough and 'B' for Blandford) reveal that some utensils belonged in the main kitchen while others were used in a separate kitchen for the Marquis of Blandford, the Duke's eldest son ▼*

*Upper Servants*
House steward
Butler
Housekeeper
Groom of the Chambers
Valet
Lady's maid
Cook
French hairdresser
Nurse
Governess

*Lower Servants*
Under butler
Footman
Housemaid
Nursery maid
Kitchen maid
Laundry maid
Dairy maid
Still-room maid
Steward's Room man/
Hall boy
Odd man / Helper

# The Still Room Maid or 'Tweenie'

The still room was originally a room in which a still was kept for the distillation of cordials. It later became a second kitchen where jams and drinks (such as tea, coffee and chocolate) were prepared. At Blenheim there was a separate bake house for making breads and cakes.

The still room maid was a member of the lower household, reporting to both the housekeeper and the cook. Since she was responsible to these two separate sections of the household, she was sometimes known as a 'Between Maid' or 'Tweenie'.

*A range of jelly moulds that were used in the still room*

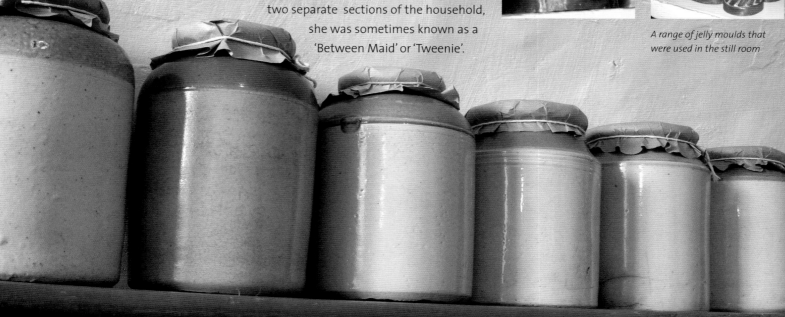

A ranger, five gamekeepers, a shepherd, a poulterer, a fisherman, and a pheasant man kept the kitchens supplied with sufficient food. A cowman and two dairy maids provided the required amounts of milk, cream and butter.

Despite the game, fish, meat, poultry and dairy products that were sourced from Blenheim Park, as well as the fruit and vegetables which were supplied from the Kitchen Garden, the estate was not entirely self-supporting. As a consequence, local tradesmen benefited, and were rarely short of business in the 4th Duke's time. The household accounts over two years show just how much was laid out to feed the family and the servants who worked for them:

*The larder accounts for the 1790s show that roughly 12,800 lbs of meat (5,818 kg) were being consumed at Blenheim every quarter, which is over 140 lbs of meat (63.6 kg) every day.*

| Kitchen expenses: | £ | s | d |
|---|---|---|---|
| **Wines** | 1,076 | 0 | 11 |
| **Coal** | 878 | 6 | 5 |
| **Candles** | 356 | 13 | 2 |
| **Poulterers** | 512 | 13 | 9¾ |
| **Butchers** | 510 | 13 | 8 |
| **Grocers** | 504 | 12 | 3 |
| **Fishmongers** | 177 | 9 | 8 |
| **Oilmen** | 116 | 2 | 3½ |
| **Cheesemongers** | 75 | 1 | 5½ |
| **Greengrocers** | 38 | 0 | 10½ |
| **Milkmen** | 31 | 15 | 1 |

# Old money - £:s:d

*Before decimalisation in 1971, the pound was divided into 20 shillings and a shilling equalled 12 pennies. The pound sign '£' derives from the letter L, for the Latin word 'Librae', while the symbol for the shilling was 's' for 'solidus' and for the penny 'd' for 'denarius'.*

*The solidus and denarius were Roman coins.*

*A guinea was £1:1s or 21 shillings.*

Apart from food and board, with the large numbers employed, the servants' annual wage bill was substantial and the cost of uniforms or liveries had to be added which made the outlay even more significant.

| Year | Wages £ | Uniforms/Liveries £ |
|------|---------|---------------------|
| 1753 | 1,046 | 734 |
| 1755 | 1,046 | – |
| 1764 | 1,675 | 1,146 |
| 1771 | 1,570 | – |
| 1772 | 1,390 | – |
| 1774 | 2,411 | 596* |
| 1787 | 1,708 | – |
| 1789 | 1,765 | – |
| 1790 | 1,786 | – |
| 1795 | 1,772 | – |
| 1816 | 1,724 | – |

*\* from this time full livery was only supplied once every two years*

*The Kitchen Garden at Blenheim was a 12-acre plot situated a short distance away from the house. The fruits and vegetables grown here were taken up to the kitchen by the head gardener every day* ▶ ◀

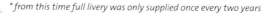

# The cost of livery...

The servants' records at Blenheim in 1787 show that a suit of livery cost £2:18:10 and consisted of a crimson cloth frockcoat, a buff cloth waistcoat and crimson shag breeches. The buttons were silver, with the family crest. If laced livery was required, it cost an extra 13 shillings. Lacing consisted of a silver braid being applied to the edges of the suit of clothes.

*Footman's dress livery* ◂

At Blenheim, the steward always ran the estate. This included the house, where the butler and the housekeeper were the most senior members of the indoor staff. The butler had to supervise all the indoor menservants. In 1775, these included a groom of the chambers, an under butler, six footmen, an usher of the hall, a steward's room man, a houseman, a helper and a cellar man. The housekeeper oversaw the women inside the house: nine different maids, as well as five laundry maids.

The butler's domain was the dining room, the wine cellar and the silver pantry while the rest of the house (bedrooms, drawing rooms, etc.) came under the direct supervision of the housekeeper. They did not have to wear uniforms or liveries. However, the records of these servants during the time of the 4th Duke throw up some interesting particulars.

In 1764, both the butler (William Barke) and the housekeeper (Elizabeth Beeston) were paid the same annual wage, £20. By 1771-2, the butler (Thomas Coles) received £45, more than double the earlier wage, while the housekeeper (Rebecca Hobson) still got the same salary, £20. In 1787 Thomas Mountney was employed as the butler at £45 but there was no housekeeper on the payroll.

## Moving on...

*When leaving service, a formal testimonial or "character" was given by an employer as to the qualities and habits of the servant. Since servants needed and were usually provided a "good character" to secure another position, testimonials became inadequate instruments in differentiating the good from the mediocre. Employers usually relied on the personal recommendations of people they knew.*

# Male Servants in the Household

The **Steward** controlled the domestic affairs of the household and regulated its expenditure. The **Butler** was in charge of the menservants in the house. He served at the dinner table and also had the responsibility of the wine cellar, the household glass and plate. Next-in-command was the **Groom of the Chambers**. In earlier times he was in charge of the furniture and furnishings in the public rooms of the house and also waited on the family. In the 19th century, he was responsible for dispatching mail from the house, ensuring that every room was stocked with paper and ink, ordering the newspapers and ironing them before the family handled them at breakfast. The **Valet** was the Duke's personal servant and looked after all his clothes, shoes and dressing requirements. The **Under Butler** was in charge of cleaning and polishing the silver. He was a liveried servant and would lay the table and also bring the food up from the kitchen to the dining room. He would be assisted by liveried Footmen. **Footmen** would also brush clothes, clean lamps and knives, answer service bells and act as valets to younger male members of the household and visiting male guests who did not bring their own staff with them.

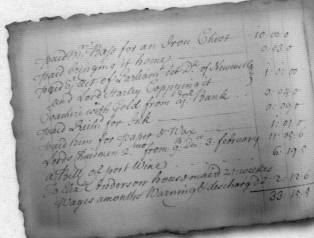

However an incident which occurred later that year shook the household and its master. A man called Thomas White, thought to be the under butler, was caught stealing plate (to the value of more than £500) from the house. Before being apprehended, he managed to sell part of the stolen silver to a man in Houndsditch, who melted it down. White was publicly hanged at Oxford Castle for this offence and Mountney, the butler, was either dismissed or left Blenheim soon afterwards.

He was replaced from the 16th of June 1789 by John Todd, at a higher wage of £50 annually, while Elena Beardmore, the newly employed housekeeper, continued to be paid at the old rate of £20. This might have provoked her into leaving within the year because, the following year, Sarah Beales was hired as housekeeper at Blenheim with an improved salary of £25, and within five years this was raised to £30.

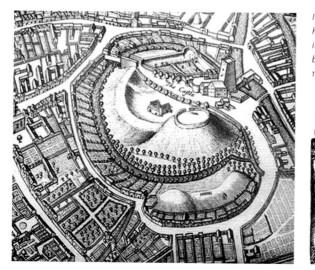

*In Oxford, the last public hanging, in the open air, was in 1863. Executions continued, behind closed doors, until the 1950s.*

# General Rates of Pay – 1812

| | £:s |
|---|---|
| Man Cook | 84:00 |
| Butler | 50:00 |
| Groom of the Chambers | – |
| Valet | – |
| Porter | 20:00 |
| Under butler | 20:00 |
| Footmen [each] | 20:00 |
| Houseman | 28:00 |
| Steward's Room Man | 18:18 |
| [of which for attending the Chaplain .... 6:06] | |
| Gardener | 50:00 |
| Coachman | 40:00 |
| Post Chaise man | 24:00 |

| | £:s |
|---|---|
| Postilion | 14:00 |
| 1st Groom | 20:00 |
| 2nd Groom | 16:00 |
| 3rd Groom | 10:00 |
| Housekeeper | 35:00 |
| Housekeeper at London | 25:00 |
| Upper Housemaids [each] | 8:00 |
| 2nd Housemaids [each] | 7:00 |
| Still Room Maids [each] | 7:00 |
| Laundry Maids [each] | 10:00 |
| Dairy Maids [each] | 8:00 |
| Woman Cook | – |
| Kitchen Maid | 8:00 |

These rates remained unchanged till the 4th Duke died in 1817.

## Smallbones

*Some servants had a long history of service under
successive generations of Marlboroughs.
Richard Smallbones was employed by Sarah, Duchess
of Marlborough at High Lodge, one of the houses on
the estate. She subsequently made him a deer keeper in
the Park, where he continued working when
Blenheim became the home of Charles Spencer, the 3rd
Duke of Marlborough, in 1744. Smallbones married
Mary Low, whose father was the gatekeeper at
Wootton. They had a large family – their youngest
child, George, was born when Smallbones was 60 and
his wife 55! Smallbones died at North Lodge in 1787,
while in the service of the 4th Duke of Marlborough.*

Another major upheaval occurred in the household when Caroline, the 4th Duchess, died in 1811. The Duke had already become quite a recluse and the upper servants appear to have assumed greater control of the household management. Quite a few servants left Blenheim during the last years of the 4th Duke's life. An examination of surviving accounts for 1795 (76 servants) and 1816 (67 servants) reveals that 17 faithful members of staff still remained in the Duke's service, but of these loyal servants, just five were indoor staff.

In general, the turnover of servants all over the country was high, and Blenheim was no exception. Servants remained for between two to three years on average, usually at the same rate of pay. Any rise in salary from one year to the next was the exception rather than the rule; the only way of increasing one's earnings was by changing employers. Promotions were also unusual, but not entirely uncommon.

At Blenheim, amazingly, two servants remained on the staff roll for over 50 years. Richard Beckley, the fisherman (who continuously earned £60 a year), and James Alderton, employed as huntsman in 1764 at £20, who rose to become head gamekeeper with a salary of £110 in the final years of the 4th Duke's life.

However, both these men were outdoor servants, and when it came to those employed inside the house, only a few remained for any considerable length of time, sometimes moving through a variety of stations: James Beckley joined the Duke's household in 1771, as second cook with an annual salary of £31:10. By 1787, he was promoted to the position of head cook (earning £73:10) and after 45 years in service, in 1816, he had risen to the post of steward, where he controlled and supervised all the staff on the estate and kept the accounts, earning £126 annually.

George Thorpe rose more conventionally through the ranks. In 1764 he joined as a footman (salary £8), by 1771 he had risen to become groom of the chambers (salary £30) and was finally butler in 1775 (salary £45) after which he left Blenheim.

Mary Meredith, was retained as a confectioner's maid, earning £6 a year in 1771. A year later her salary was increased to £9 and by 1787 she had become housekeeper, with an annual wage of £20.

# Perks

*Certain servants received perquisites that went with their positions.*

*For example, cooks were able to sell the fat from the kitchen to the tallow chandler, maids received their mistress's cast off clothes (to wear or sell as they pleased), and the butler got the ends of wax candles as well as empty bottles which he sold, keeping the money he received.*

Ann Brown was employed as plate maid in 1771 (salary £6) and held the same post for many years till 1787 when she took over as the nurse at a salary of £16:16. Her wages were raised to £21 in 1790 and, after 24 years in the family's service, in 1795 she was promoted to the position of governess, earning £26.

There were several shorter career progressions where footmen (£8) became porters (£20) or gatekeepers (£25) or valets (£31-36); and housemaids (£6) became laundry maids (£8). Sometimes housemaids were moved around between the various houses owned by the Duke and from 1787 there was a designated position of travelling maid, a housemaid who accompanied the family wherever they went.

Although the wages of these servants appear meagre, they were the norm in the context of working class incomes at the time and were seen as attractive when the value of a room and board was added (paid for by the employer), along with tips and other perquisites that went with certain posts.

Salary levels hardly increased through the 18th century. In the early 1700s, a housemaid employed by Sarah, 1st Duchess of Marlborough would have received £6 annually. At Blenheim, the same wage

*The Kitchen Court at Blenheim Palace* ▽

was paid to housemaids until 1789 when the rate was increased to £7, or sometimes £8, in the time of Caroline, 4th Duchess of Marlborough.

What is most notable however, in studying these accounts, is the widening gap between the wages earned by men compared to women. By the 19th century, domestic service had substantially become a female occupation. One factor in tipping the balance was that in 1781, the government introduced a new tax on male servants. This measure was a further burden on the wealthier classes, who were already paying a variety of levies – on their houses, on the number of windows and, from 1747, on their coaches. The resultant shift from employing men to women grew steadily from 1780 to 1820 and reached its peak in the Victorian and Edwardian periods.

28
29
30
31
32

*Yellow Damask Dressing-Room*

*Gun Room.*

*Saloon*

33
34
35

1817-1857
Introducing efficiency

ITH TAXATION STEADILY ON THE RISE, when the 5th Duke took over the Blenheim estate on his father's death, his bill of levies made interesting reading:

The 5th Duke and Duchess

|  | £ | s | d |  | £ | s | d |
|---|---|---|---|---|---|---|---|
| Windows | 181 | 18 | 6 | 4 wheel carriages | 42 | 0 | 0 |
| Inhabited rent | 42 | 10 | 0 | Horses for riding | 123 | 10 | 0 |
| Male Servants | 225 | 11 | 0 | Other horses | 32 | 11 | 0 |
| Hair powder | 10 | 11 | 6 | Dogs | 30 | 14 | 0 |
| Armorial bearings | 8 | 0 | 0 | Total | **£691** | **14** | **0** |

From the 1820s onwards, retrenchment was the order of the day. The 5th Duke's profligacy had resulted in serious financial difficulty for the estate. Staff numbers were cut back. The lax regime run by the upper servants after the 4th Duchess's death was quickly brought under control by Susan, wife of the 5th Duke.

# RULES TO BE STRICTLY OBSERVED

☞ *The servants are all to dine at one o'clock, before the Parlour dinner, both Upper and Under Servants, and to breakfast and sup at nine - & no <u>hot</u> suppers.*

☞ *The Butler, or Groom of the Chambers, to see that the Servants Hall and <u>Powder Rooms</u> are cleaned and locked up ever night <u>before</u> 11 o'clock.*

☞ *<u>All</u> the Servants to sleep in the House when the Family is at Blenheim; unless with special leave for any particular caus*

☞ *The Under Butler to be assisted by all the Footmen in turns as there will be no Plate Maid.*

☞ *The plate to be washed by the 2nd Stillroom maid, and in the Stillroom; from whence the Under Butler must fetch it.*

☞ *The plate to be kept and <u>cleaned in the Pantry</u>, and the present dark plate room to be shut up.*

☞ *All the Glass etc. to be kept in the waiting room and closets adjoining; and to be cleared out of the dining room every day after dinner.*

☞ *The Butler to keep the key and take charge of the Ale Cellars; also to superintend <u>all</u> the Under menservants, and to keep the Accounts, passing them all with Mr Fellows.*

☞ *No meals to be allowed anywhere, excepting the Servants Hall and Stewards room.  Breakfast excepted.*

☞ *<u>No</u> garden men or milkmen to have their meals here.*

☞ *No Posthorses or <u>hacks</u> to be taken into the stables, being so near Woodstock.*

☞ *Should any objections be made to these reforms, <u>those</u> persons may retire.*

LENHEIM HAD ALREADY COME TO NOTICE in high society as being *"worse even than the common run of bad great houses – they kill two oxen and twenty sheep a week, and the waste, riot and drunkenness that go forward from morning to night are sufficient to demoralise any neighbourhood."* The new Duchess introduced strict rules for the servants, which she wrote out herself, to rein in offensive habits that had grown in the absence of a mistress in the house.

Some of the servants employed by the 4th Duke remained at Blenheim, but the greater part were either replaced or let go. From 37 indoor servants in the last year of the 4th Duke's life, the 5th Duke reduced numbers to 25, retaining 19 of his father's servants when he took over in 1817. As time moved on and his debts mounted, numbers were cut back further to just 15 servants in 1821. Four men and three women who had served under his father survived these cuts:

| | |
|---|---|
| **John Bartlett** | – *Butler* |
| **Martin Maylard** | – *Porter* |
| **John Slatter** | – *Steward's Room Man* |
| **William Hanks** | – *Footman, who in 1817 became the 5th Duke's valet* |
| **Susan Hanks** | – *Kitchen maid, who in 1817 took over as woman cook* |
| **Mary Rymill** | – *Laundry maid* |
| **Elizabeth Shepherd** | – *Still room maid, who in 1821 became a general housemaid* |

*Porter's canopied armchair, c. 1860 in George II style. This chair was used by the porter on door-opening duty. The tall arched canopy, covered in red morocco leather and embossed with the Marlborough coat of arms, helped to exclude draughts. The mahogany cabriole legs of the chair are carved with foliage and terminate in claw and ball feet.*

*The Porters' chairs at Blenheim Palace are of exceptional height – 6ft 7½ in. (202cm) – in keeping with the lofty proportions of the Great Hall ▶*

Thomas Beckley, the 4th Duke's under butler who had left his service at the end of the 1790s returned to Blenheim as footman in 1817. However, he left again within a short time as the 5th Duke was unable to pay his servants' wages. Bailiffs had already called a number of times to seize goods in settlement of tax bills and by April 1821, most of the servants were owed two to three years' wages. They still had a roof over their heads and food on the table, but depended largely on tips from visitors until their dues were paid. A guest in 1827 disclosed just how dire the situation was *"as we entered... some very dirty servants ran past us to fetch the chatelaine...she required that we should inscribe our names in a large book: unhappily however, there was no ink in the inkstand."*

◀ *The front door to Blenheim Palace and* ▲ *the huge knocker in the shape of a Green Man*

*The front door key, engraved with the words 'SERVANT KEY, ENTRANCE DOORS, BLENHEIM'* ▼

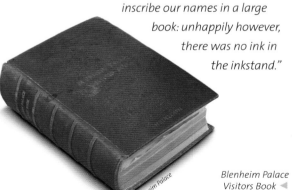

*Blenheim Palace Visitors Book* ◀

Despite the Duke's financial difficulties, grand parties were still held. On these occasions servants were instructed to light lamps all around the Great Court and stable hands were in position at the base of the main steps to lead guests' coaches away as they arrived at the front door. Dinner was served by the butler at precisely 5.30pm, and two servants were on duty all evening to attend to the candles throughout the house. Wax candles were always used inside the house while the staff areas were lit with tallow candles and oil lamps. This tradition continued until the installation of gas lamps.

Progress had also been made on another front when mechanical sweepers were introduced in 1803 and the climbing boys used by chimney sweeps prohibited from 1829 onwards. Useful modernisation in other areas of the house was to follow not long afterwards.

© Blenheim Palace

▼ *A 19th-century hanging lantern and a bronze gasolier c. 1825, both now converted to electricity* ◀

▶ *A Blenheim Palace chimney board, linking each chimney on the roof to a room in the house*

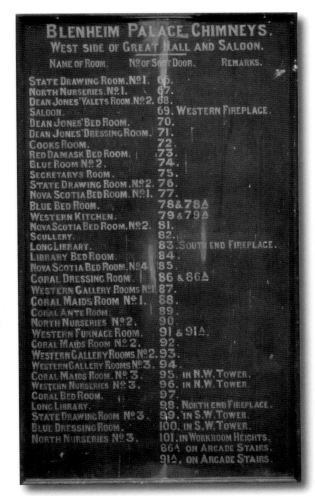

| BLENHEIM PALACE, CHIMNEYS. | | |
|---|---|---|
| WEST SIDE OF GREAT HALL AND SALOON. | | |
| NAME OF ROOM. | № OF SOOT DOOR. | REMARKS. |
| STATE DRAWING ROOM. № 1. | 66. | |
| NORTH NURSERIES. № 1. | 67. | |
| DEAN JONES' VALETS ROOM. № 2. | 68. | |
| SALOON. | 69. | WESTERN FIREPLACE. |
| DEAN JONES' BED ROOM. | 70. | |
| DEAN JONES' DRESSING ROOM. | 71. | |
| COOKS ROOM. | 72. | |
| RED DAMASK BED ROOM. | 73. | |
| BLUE ROOM № 2. | 74. | |
| SECRETARY'S ROOM. | 75. | |
| STATE DRAWING ROOM. № 2. | 76. | |
| NOVA SCOTIA BED ROOM. № 1. | 77. | |
| BLUE BED ROOM. | 78 & 78A. | |
| WESTERN KITCHEN. | 79 & 79A. | |
| NOVA SCOTIA BED ROOM. № 2. | 81. | |
| SCULLERY. | 82. | |
| LONG LIBRARY. | 83. | SOUTH END FIREPLACE. |
| LIBRARY BED ROOM. | 84. | |
| NOVA SCOTIA BED ROOM. № 4. | 85. | |
| CORAL DRESSING ROOM. | 86 & 86A. | |
| WESTERN GALLERY ROOMS № 1. | 87. | |
| CORAL MAIDS ROOM № 1. | 88. | |
| CORAL ANTE ROOM. | 89. | |
| NORTH NURSERIES № 2. | 90. | |
| WESTERN FURNACE ROOM. | 91 & 91A. | |
| CORAL MAIDS ROOM № 2. | 92. | |
| WESTERN GALLERY ROOMS № 2. | 93. | |
| WESTERN GALLERY ROOMS № 3. | 94. | |
| CORAL MAIDS ROOM № 3. | 95. | IN N.W. TOWER. |
| WESTERN NURSERIES № 3. | 96. | IN N.W. TOWER. |
| CORAL BED ROOM. | 97. | |
| LONG LIBRARY. | 98. | NORTH END FIREPLACE. |
| STATE DRAWING ROOM № 3. | 99. | IN S.W. TOWER. |
| BLUE DRESSING ROOM. | 100. | IN S.W. TOWER. |
| NORTH NURSERIES № 3. | 101. | IN WORKROOM HEIGHTS. |
| | 86A. | ON ARCADE STAIRS. |
| | 91A. | ON ARCADE STAIRS. |

The old kitchen in the Kitchen Court was a long way away from the dining room on the principal floor of the main body of the house. The long passages linking the kitchen to the dining room made it impossible to have hot food served at the table. The earlier 18th-century concerns for the smells of food from the kitchen, as well as the risks of a fire being started there, had lessened by the time the 6th Duke occupied the house (1840-1857). The kitchens were moved out of the Kitchen Court to the undercroft [basement] below the main house itself. New ovens that controlled temperatures more effectively were installed to lessen the risk of fire and cast iron pans replaced the earlier copper utensils. A new enclosed staircase was built in the central open courtyard of the east wing to provide direct access from the new kitchens to the dining room.

By 1844, the dairy was moved to the Kitchen Court where the laundry had once been. A large fountain, built in artificial stone by John Seeley, was installed in the centre of the

*The 6th Duke*

*The new enclosed staircase built by the 6th Duke provided direct access from the new kitchens to the dining room.* ▼

*The open arcaded servants' corridor under the east colonnade which linked the old kitchen to the main block of the house* ◄

© Andrew Esson

*A fountain was placed in the dairy to keep milk and butter cool. Details on the side of the top basin include two panels carved with cows – appropriate symbolism for the dairy. This fountain, made in artificial stone by John Seeley, was delivered in February 1843 and cost £120.* ►►

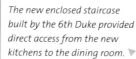

© Blenheim Palace to left and right

new dairy to cool butter and milk. The walls of the room were half-tiled. A new cheese room was created in the old drying yard and the dairy maids were given their own sitting room.

On the opposite side of the Kitchen Court, the open yard adjacent to the old kitchen was enclosed and converted into new offices for the Duke, the steward and several clerks. For the next 150 years, the estate was administered from here. The old kitchen was transformed into the audit room where the estate's tenants would come to pay the rent.

In the early 1850s, the 6th Duke also installed a gas works outside the Stable Court to bring the modern comfort of underfloor heating to some of Blenheim's principal rooms and main corridors. This system was made redundant in the late 1880s when it was replaced by the 8th Duke.

*The Victorian etched glass panel of the old Estate Office door.* ◄

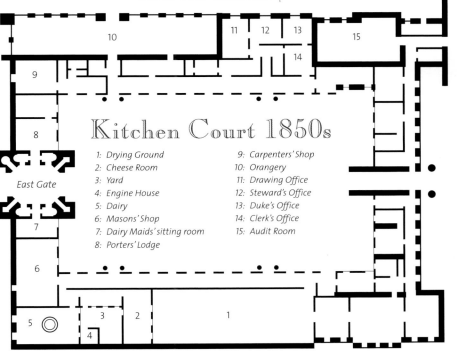

## Kitchen Court 1850s

1: Drying Ground
2: Cheese Room
3: Yard
4: Engine House
5: Dairy
6: Masons' Shop
7: Dairy Maids' sitting room
8: Porters' Lodge
9: Carpenters' Shop
10: Orangery
11: Drawing Office
12: Steward's Office
13: Duke's Office
14: Clerk's Office
15: Audit Room

East Gate

1857-1934
Modernisation and innovation

THE 7TH DUKE REAWAKENED THE HOUSE with a family of eleven children and Victorian high society living.

*The 7th Duke*

In 1871, the Housekeeper was Mary Ann Sessions, a 34-year-old widow from Lambeth. She supervised three lady's maids, six housemaids, three laundry maids, and a dairymaid. The kitchen was run by a French chef, Mr Hasnal, assisted by two kitchen maids. In high society, employing a French chef added a certain prestige to the table. There were nine male servants in the house, including two valets, two footmen, a porter and a groom of the chambers.

*The east wing of Blenheim from 'Vitruvius Britannicus'* ◀

© Blenheim Palace

*The 8th Duke and Duchess*

WHEN THE 7TH DUKE WAS APPOINTED Lord Lieutenant (Viceroy) of Ireland in 1876, the family moved to Dublin and Blenheim was looked after by a skeleton staff for about four years while he remained in office. During this period, and whenever the family were away, household servants were paid board wages, to cover the cost of their food.

When it was built, Blenheim was at the forefront of modernity, with a piped water supply. Water from the river was pumped up to a cistern installed in the Kitchen Court tower from where it fed the east wing of the house. However, although Sarah, the 1st Duchess had her own bathing room in the

*Victorian light fitting* ▲

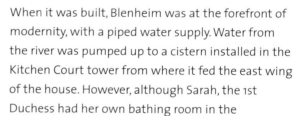

*Victorian washstand with marble surround and a range of toilet wares made by Copeland, with the ducal coronet and 'M' for Marlborough in gold* ▲

# Board Wages

*During the time of the 1st Duchess, the servants that travelled with her did not have board wages and those that lived at her country houses only had board wages when she left. She recorded that her "ordinary maid servants in the country have but 5 shillings a week board wages [at] Windsor and [at] Blenheim; because they have the advantage of what they want of the dairy things, and the board wages of the porters and grooms left in the country is 7 shillings a week".*

*By the end of the 19th century, in the 9th Duke's time, the board wages paid to servants were in the order of 12 shillings a week, plus vegetables, milk and half a pound of butter each.*

undercroft [basement] below her bedchamber, no other bathrooms existed in the house for over a century, until some were put in by the 8th Duke in the late 1880s after his second marriage to the American heiress, Lilian Hammersley. Her money also allowed for electric lighting to be introduced to the house.

By 1896 the modern conveniences of electricity and telephone had been installed at Blenheim. There were four electricians employed at this time, all highly valued and important members of staff.

The dairy in the north-east corner of the Kitchen Court, which still maintained the tradition of producing butter and cream for the entire household, was also electrified with its own engine house in the adjacent yard.

*These cleverly-disguised and impressive radiators were installed in the east wing when the central heating system was modernised in the late 1880s* ▶

© Blenheim Palace

*In the 18th century, servants were summoned by hand bells* ▲

Servants in the early 18th century were more visible and needed to be close at hand as, initially, the only way of getting assistance was by calling out or by using a hand bell. The invention of the bell-pull in the early 19th century changed the way the household operated. Through a system of wires which ran through wall and ceiling cavities, bells could be rung upstairs to summon the

*The mid 19th century bell board installed in the undercroft. Each bell was rung by turning the corresponding handle in an 'upstairs' room* ▲◄

The bell rang on the board downstairs when the corresponding handle was turned in the room upstairs. When the bell stopped ringing, the pendulum above it would continue to swing, allowing the servants a few extra minutes to reach the board to see where they were required. An experienced servant would often recognize the bell by its tone, because every one had a different timbre ▲

These 'modern' wire operated indicator panels replaced the old bell board at Blenheim Palace by the turn of the 20th century ▲▼

Early internal telephone system installed by the 8th Duke ▲◄

servants from downstairs or other distant parts of the house. Servants now became even more invisible than before. This system only became defunct with the invention and introduction of the telephone. There were 37 telephone lines connecting the 8th Duke to various offices around the house and estate, with a young hall-boy manning the switchboard.

The 9th Duke

THE 9TH DUKE'S AMERICAN WIFE, Consuelo Vanderbilt, found the conventions and routines of the English country household wearisome. In her account of her life at Blenheim from 1895 to 1905, she observed the complex system of etiquette below stairs: *"A strange ritual took place in the servant's hall. The under servants first trooped in and remained standing at their places until the upper servants had filed in in order of domestic status. After the first course the upper servants left in the following manner: When the joint, carved by the house steward, had been eaten and second helpings offered, it was ceremoniously removed by the steward's room footman, who carried it out with great pomp, followed by the upper servants who then retired to the steward's room for the remainder of their meal; while the housemaids and sewing-maids scurried off with platefuls of pudding to eat in their own sitting rooms."* Everyday matters like eating places and dress constantly reinforced the distinction between upper and lower servants.

During house parties, visiting servants created even more work for the household staff. A strict hierarchy operated below stairs. At Blenheim, visiting valets and lady's maids took their meals in the steward's room where they were called by their master's names and took their places at the servant's table in order of their master's ranks. There were well established orders of precedence and deference that operated both above and below stairs.

The 9th Duchess

© Blenheim Palace

# Chapel Services

A bell would be rung to call the household together for a weekly service. During the 4th Duke's time, these were held in the Chapel at 3 pm every Sunday afternoon. This was a day and time at which no outside visitors except the family's guests were allowed on the estate.

Later, in the Victorian household of the 7th Duke, daily morning prayers were held in the Chapel. This tradition continued through to the 9th Duke's period with prayers in the Chapel at 9.30 every morning. Consuelo, Duchess of Marlborough recalls in her memoirs that *"at the toll of the bell housemaids would drop their dusters, footmen their trays, housemaids their pails, laundry maids their linen and all rush to reach the Chapel in time. Heads of Departments had already taken their seats in the pews allotted for them."*

© Andrew Esson

At the end of the 19th century, footmen were only employed at Blenheim if they were more than 6 feet tall. They had to wear livery and powder their hair. This was a laborious process which involved washing the hair with soap, combing it out and powdering it with a mix of Violet powder and flour so that it set rock hard and completely white. Blenheim Palace footmen received a powdering allowance of 2 guineas a year to purchase Violet powder for this process.

The uniforms for liveried footmen consisted of the family colours – maroon breeches and coat with a crested silver buttoned waistcoat, edged with silver lace [braid]. Flesh coloured silk stockings were worn with black patent shoes with silver buckles. The maids' uniform consisted of a plain black dress.

In the early 20th century, six housemaids worked at Blenheim Palace under the supervision of the housekeeper. There were five laundry maids and a still room maid, who now also cooked the breakfasts and made the cakes and scones for afternoon tea. At this time, the still room was located near the south eastern corner of the undercroft.

The kitchen itself was managed by a French chef with a staff of four. All meat dishes were provided by this kitchen, which made the serving of breakfasts extremely fraught. Consuelo, the wife of the 9th Duke, recalled that the food was often served cold.

The lodge-keepers or gate porters also had to be over six foot in height. Their uniform consisted of black coats with crested silver buttons, buff breeches and gaiters. They wore a cockaded top hat and carried a silver-topped staff.

*A gate porter at Blenheim Palace c. 1900* ▶

There are four Flags, viz.--Storm Flag, Pennant, Large Flag with Coat-of-Arms, and the Union Jack.

The Flag is to be hoisted every day when the Duke or Duchess of Marlborough are at home: at the hour of Eight a.m. in Summer and Nine a.m. in Winter.

The Flag is to be hauled down at sun-set always.

The Storm Flag is to be used on all days with High Wind or Rain of a heavy nature.

The Pennant is to be hoisted on all moderately fine days, and is in fact the Principal Flag to be used.

The Union Jack is to be hoisted on all fine bright warm days, and can be changed if the weather turns into a bad afternoon with Wind and Rain.

The Large Flag with Coat-of-Arms is only to be hoisted on special occasions, and only in fine weather.

The Porter is responsible for the charge of the Flags, and seeing to their being sent to the Office for repairs.

**MARLBOROUGH.**

*The gate porter on duty at the east gate was also responsible for the daily ritual of hoisting the flag according to the Flag Rules (above). The large flag with the coat of arms is still used on special occasions* ◀

During the hundreds of years that the Marlborough family has lived at Blenheim, certain individuals have been employed from time to time to carry out somewhat quaint, curious or uncommon duties.

The 1st Duke was attended by a man who helped him clean his teeth, and by a woman called Mrs Jones who, in 1718, was paid ten guineas to dress his blisters! A dancing master was employed for his children while later in the 18th century, the 4th Duke employed "two French Horns".

The 4th Duke also employed a running footman. This was usually a servant who had a splendid physique and was hired to run alongside his master's carriage. He assisted by supporting the side of the coach, especially when making turns, to prevent it from toppling. The first running footman recorded at Blenheim Palace was Frederick Beihel (from 1787 to 1790), and afterwards James Phillips till 1795. It is said that one of the 4th Duke's running footmen died of exhaustion after a competition was arranged, pitting him in a race against the

horse-drawn coach between London and Windsor. It is possible that the man who died was James Philips, as there are no further records of running footmen in the surviving documents, and it is presumed the position lapsed on account of this tragedy.

Amongst the more unusual workers hired by the 9th Duke was a cricket coach who instructed him and his sons. Two wine specialists came in once a week to stock both the champagne and wine cellars. There was also a week-end visitor in the form of Mr Perkins, the organist, who came down regularly from Birmingham to play the organ in the library for the family after dinner. These individuals were not considered to be servants in the traditional sense of the word. However, the two house electricians, who were counted as servants, were the equals of the butler in status and were treated with the respect due to 'men of science'.

© Blenheim Palace

In 1896, a day after the Prince of Wales (the future King Edward VII) and the royal shooting party had left Blenheim, a fire broke out in the roof of the Saloon. The Blenheim Fire Brigade, luckily on practice that day, was summoned within five minutes. The Brigade consisted of 13 members of the household staff – two gate porters, the electric-light engineer, the Palace stoker, the gas-and-waterman and his assistant (both these men were called "odd-men" and lived inside the house in Bachelor's Row), the second coachman and six men from the garden. The Brigade was supervised by the butler.

The Fire Engine itself was steam powered and was the responsibility of the Engineer. The water for the engine was supplied from the reservoirs at High Lodge (a small house on the estate) to hydrants both inside and outside the Palace. The gas-and-waterman was responsible for the maintenance of these hydrants. The Rules explain *"to work each hydrant, take off cap, affix and run out canvas hose where required, screw on branch pipe, lay same on ground or floor, then open valve and direct the jet on the fire."* The Fire Engine was capable of pumping 60,000 gallons of water every hour. On this occasion, the fire was successfully put out and the insurance company rewarded each member of the brigade staff with £5.

A previous fire, which broke out on 5th February 1861 in the north block of the Kitchen Court completely destroyed the interiors of those rooms. It was after this disastrous event that Blenheim's staff were trained to form their own Fire Brigade.

*High Lodge in Blenheim Park. In the 8th Duke's time, the Woodman and Park Keeper lived in this house on the estate. It was also used by the family and their guests as a picnic and stopping point during winter shooting parties* ◀

### The Odd Man

*With the advent of central heating and piped hot water in the 1880-90s during the tenure of the 8th Duke, the position of 'Odd Man' was first recorded at Blenheim Palace designating the person who looked after the coal-fired boiler in the Stable Court. He would also stock each bedroom with coal for the housemaids to lay the fires as well as being called on to do other odd jobs like washing windows, carrying luggage or water to the bedrooms, and chopping wood for the log baskets in the Saloon.*

# The Blenheim Fire Brigade

In 1842 Blenheim was equipped with a fire engine costing about £180, bought from Thomas Jones & Sons. This was replaced in 1899 by a new Merryweather & Sons steam fire engine for which £451:13:4 was paid. Merryweather's engine was designed with an innovative vertical boiler system, which improved the water pressure pumped by the engine. It ran with special firewood supplied by W H Branch. In 1903, Merryweather also supplied uniforms for the Blenheim Fire Brigade at a cost of £35. The firemen were members of the household staff who together received a supplement for this additional duty amounting to roughly £30-35 a year.

*The new Merryweather fire engine* ▲ *and fire-fighting equipment inside the Palace.* ▼

*A group photo of the expanded Blenheim fire brigade with both fire engines when the new*

*Merryweather engine was delivered in January 1899* ▼

# The Stable Court 1890s

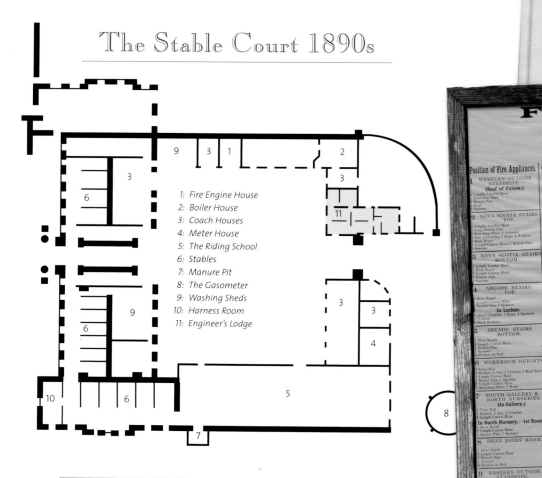

1: Fire Engine House
2: Boiler House
3: Coach Houses
4: Meter House
5: The Riding School
6: Stables
7: Manure Pit
8: The Gasometer
9: Washing Sheds
10: Harness Room
11: Engineer's Lodge

**MERRYWEATHER & SONS'**
**FIRE RULES**
FOR PRIVATE RESIDENCES.

## FIRE RULES.

### BLENHEIM PALACE.

**ORDERS RELATING TO FIRE ENGINES AND APPLIANCES.**

The HOUSE BUTLER has the chief control of the fire arrangements.

The FIRE BRIGADE will consist of the Two Gate Porters, the Electric-Light Engineer, the Palace Stoker and the Two Odd Men, the Gas and Waterman, and his Assistant, (who will live in Bachelor's Row,) the Second Coachman, and Six Men from the Garden Bothy.

The Gas and Waterman, and his Assistant are acquainted with all Outer Hydrants.

The Outside Hydrants are all painted white.

The Thirteen men comprising the Brigade know all about the Outside Hydrants, and the Fire Engine, and House Hydrants.

A particular day is to be fixed for exercising the Brigade every month; but the Butler will, Two or Three times in the year, call an Extra Practice, without notice, (after dark, if advisable,) by permission of the Agent, in order to prove the efficiency of the Brigade.

The Hydrants in the House are fitted with Canvas Hose, and Branch Pipes, and the Housemaids will be shown how to use them in an emergency.

An Axe and Iron Crowbar are hung on the Wall on each Staircase of the House, also a Rope.

The Leather Hose is under the charge and responsibility of the Gas and Waterman. The Steam Fire Engine is under the charge of the Engineer. Keys of the Engine Houses hang in the Box on Wall outside.

The Gas and Waterman is responsible for all Hydrants, and lives at the Woodstock Mill.

A Table of Valves hangs in each Engine House, under charge of Waterman, and corresponds with the Table of Valves at the Reservoirs, and also with the Table in the High Lodge.

The Woodman and Park Keeper, who live at the High Lodge, are acquainted with the use of the Reservoir Valves, so that the orders can be sent them through the telephone or otherwise.

A small Plan of the Hydrants outside the Palace hangs in the Butler's Room.

A printed set of these Rules hangs by each Hydrant in the Palace.

To work each Hydrant, take off Cap, affix and run out Canvas Hose where required, screw on Branch Pipe, lay same on ground or floor, then open Valve and direct the jet on the fire.

In the early 1900s, the inside staff at Blenheim numbered 36-40 out of a total number of 80-90 employees. Most servants still worked long hours, the average day being 7am to 11pm, with two afternoons and evenings off a week.

After the First World War, domestic servants became harder to find throughout the country. This was especially true for the numerous young women who had previously been attracted by the security and higher standards of living obtained through such employment, but had discovered a variety of other more congenial and better paid types of work during the war, which made them reluctant to return to domestic service.

By 1919, however, the heyday of country house living (with large numbers of servants being employed) had passed. Income tax, land tax and other charges stripped roughly 30% of the wealth generated by privileged upper class estates, and death duties were raised to 40% on assets valued at over £2 million. Large country houses were increasingly in danger of extinction. The 9th Duke of Marlborough writing in *The Times* in 1920, observed that *"The old order is doomed"*.

*Plan of the Stable Court where
the fire engine was housed* ◀ ◀

*Fire Rules displayed inside
the Palace* ◀

*Between 1918 and 1945, over 400 country houses were demolished, and although the 1931 census recorded 1,300,000 women and 80,000 men working as domestic servants, the majority of these were employed by the rising number of urban middle class households.*

AT BLENHEIM PALACE, BETWEEN THE WARS, staff numbers still remained high. After the 10th Duke took over in 1934, there was a butler, an under butler, a groom of the chambers, four footmen, two odd men, a housekeeper, six maids, a French chef, kitchen maids and two still room maids. The French chef earned £260, while, at the other end of the scale, various maids were on around £50 a year.

*The 10th Duke and Duchess*

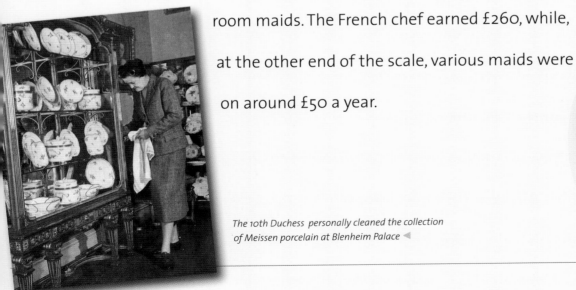

*The 10th Duchess personally cleaned the collection of Meissen porcelain at Blenheim Palace* ◄

WHEN TED WADMAN ARRIVED at Blenheim Palace in 1936 as under butler (salary £78), he recalled that the beer did not flow as freely as he might have wished as Mr Taylor, the then butler, believed there was "plenty of water in the tap". In 1947, after the war, Wadman returned to Blenheim, this time as butler with a salary of over £400 a year.

The Second World War marked the point of no return for the old way of life. When the war ended in 1945, Clement Atlee's newly elected labour government put further pressure on privilege and inherited wealth. Owners of large houses had to make difficult choices – to sell up, to pass their estates on to conservationist institutions like the National Trust, or to somehow survive in a completely changed economic and social climate. When the government offered fiscal advantages if a property remained open for at least 36 days a year, a number of owners of stately homes, including the Marlboroughs at Blenheim,

*Ted Wadman, the butler, with three footmen, cleaning silver in the pantry* ▲

*Tom Jakeman, the boilerman, was in charge of running the generator that provided electric lighting in the Palace. He had to work unsociable hours whenever there was a party in the house or when a regular visitor, Winston Churchill, cousin of the 9th Duke of Marlborough, had one of his habitual late evenings with friends in the Library* ◄

*View of the saloon with the table laid. The family no longer dines here, except at Christmas, when the house is closed to the public* ▶

chose the last option and, in April 1950, the 10th Duke opened his doors to a fee-paying public.

This innovative commercial enterprise called for a completely different mix of staff and a new flexibility in running the house. Although still very much a private home, albeit run on a more modest scale, visitors' needs now superseded those of the family.

For the past 50 years, successive Dukes have overseen the running of the estate but successive managers have made the rules, and although the butler regularly lays the silver on the state dining table, the meal never ever follows.

The Marlboroughs, having survived at Blenheim for 300 years despite the accession of profligate heirs, the sale of their finest heirlooms and an uncertain future in the face of great agricultural, economic and social change, confidently continue as custodians of their ancestral home, running it with the help of a number of dedicated staff.

*On one record day, 6,300 visitors came through the house.*

William "Taffy" Jones, one of Blenheim's longest serving modern-day members of staff. Taffy joined as Gateman in April 1972 and retired in 1997. He was re-employed on a seasonal basis thereafter, manning the entrance to the Maze. Still in service after 35 years, he now works part-time (on weekends) operating the wheelchair lift ▲

# Timeline

| Monarchs | | Dukes of Marlborough | |
|---|---|---|---|
| Anne | 1702-1714 | John, 1st Duke | 1702-1722 |
| George I | 1714-1727 | Henrietta, 2nd Duchess | 1722-1733 |
| George II | 1727-1760 | Charles, 3rd Duke | 1733-1758 |
| George III | 1760-1820 | George, 4th Duke | 1758-1817 |
| George IV | 1820-1830 | George, 5th Duke | 1817-1840 |
| William IV | 1830-1837 | George, 6th Duke | 1840-1857 |
| Victoria | 1837-1901 | John, 7th Duke | 1857-1883 |
| | | George, 8th Duke | 1883-1892 |
| Edward VII | 1901-1910 | Charles, 9th Duke | 1892-1934 |
| George V | 1910-1936 | John, 10th Duke | 1934-1972 |
| Edward VIII | 1936 | John, 11th Duke | 1972- |
| George VI | 1936-1952 | | |
| Elizabeth II | 1952- | | |

1700s

1800s

1900s

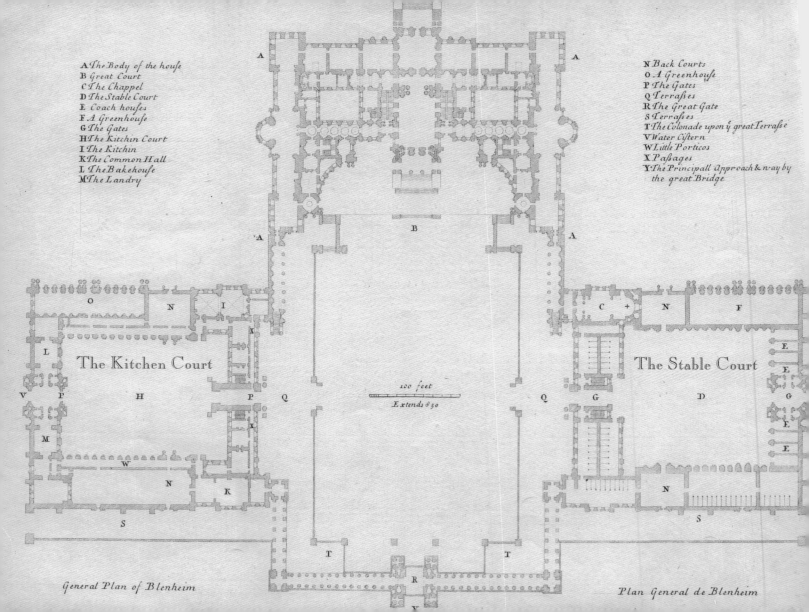

A The Body of the house
B Great Court
C The Chappel
D The Stable Court
E Coach houses
F A Greenhouse
G The Gates
H The Kitchin Court
I The Kitchin
K The Common Hall
L The Bakehouse
M The Landry

N Back Courts
O A Greenhouse
P The Gates
Q Terrasses
R The Great Gate
S Terrasses
T The Colonade upon ÿ great Terrasse
V Water Cistern
W Litle Porticos
X Passages
Y The Principall Approach & way by
   the great Bridge

The Kitchen Court

The Stable Court

100 feet
Extends 850

General Plan of Blenheim

Plan General de Blenheim